MAPS

Pebble®

Symbols and Keys

by
Jennifer M. Besel

Consulting editor:
Gail Saunders-Smith, PhD

Consultant:
Dr. Sarah E. Battersby
Department of Geography
University of South Carolina

94	INTERSTATE
41	U.S. HIGHWAY
33	STATE HIGHWAY
110	COUNTY ROAD
🌲	PARKS
	REST AREA
🚐	SERVICE AREA
	INTERSTATE HIGHWAY
	TOLL HIGHWAY
	DIVIDED HIGHWAY
	HIGHWAY
⊛	STATE CAPITAL
○	OTHER CITY

CAPSTONE PRESS
a capstone imprint

Pebble Books are published by Capstone Press,
1710 Roe Crest Drive, North Mankato, Minnesota 56003
www.capstonepub.com

Library of Congress Cataloging-in-Publication Data
Besel, Jennifer M.
Symbols and keys / by Jennifer M. Besel.
pages. cm.—(Pebble Books. Maps)
Includes bibliographical references and index.
Summary: "Simple text with full-color photos and illustrations provide basic
information about map symbols and keys"—Provided by publisher.
ISBN 978-1-4765-3082-6 (library binding)—ISBN 978-1-4765-3504-3 (ebook pdf)—
ISBN 978-1-4765-3522-7 (paperback)
1. Maps—Symbols—Juvenile literature. 2. Map scales—Juvenile literature. I. Title.
GA155B47 2014
912.01'48—dc23   2012046452

Editorial Credits
Gene Bentdahl, designer; Kathy McColley, production specialist; Sarah Schuette,
photo stylist; Marcy Morin, scheduler

Photo Credits
Capstone: 7, 9, 11, 13, 15 (top), 17, 19, 21; Capstone Studio: Karon Dubke, cover, 1, 5,
15 (bottom)

Note to Parents and Teachers

The Maps set supports social studies standards related to people, places, and
environments. This book describes and illustrates map symbols and keys. The
images support early readers in understanding the text. The repetition of words
and phrases helps early readers learn new words. This book also introduces early
readers to subject-specific vocabulary words, which are defined in the Glossary
section. Early readers may need assistance to read some words and to use the Table

MAPS

Table of Contents

Shapes on a Map

Maps have funny shapes
all over them. What are
those shapes?
They're map symbols,
and they are helpful map tools.

Sakatah Singing Hills

TRAIL OVERVIEW

Faribault

Waterville

Sakatah Lake State Park

Mankato

Eagle Lake

Wasena

Okahosha

MAP KEY

- Sakatah
- Other Bike
- Sakatah Trail
- Parks/Recreation
- Wetlands
- Parking
- Information
- Seasonal Restroom
- Food Services
- Camping
- Picnic Area
- Lodging
- Historic Site
- Fishing Pier
- Swimming
- Hospital
- Point of Interest

MANKATO TO MADISON LAKE

Mankato Municipal Airport

(Mankato)

Madison Lake

Mankato

Eagle Lake

MANKATO (at trailhead)

Maps show places on Earth.

But to make the places fit

on a small map,

mapmakers use symbols.

Symbols are shapes

that stand for real things.

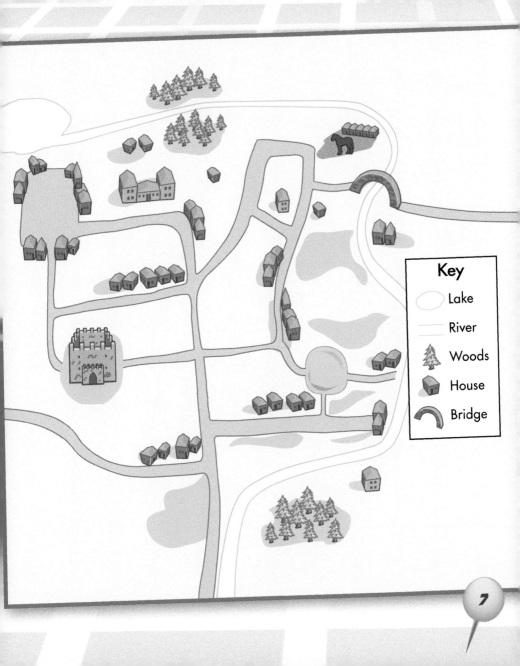

Key

◯ Lake

— River

🌲 Woods

🏠 House

🌉 Bridge

Each map has a chart

that tells what

the symbols mean.

This chart is called

a key or legend.

Key

Bike path

Post office

Library

Hospital

Fire station

Police station

School

Town hall

Downtown

Parking

Shape Symbols

Some maps use shape symbols.

A circle might be a town.

A square could be a building.

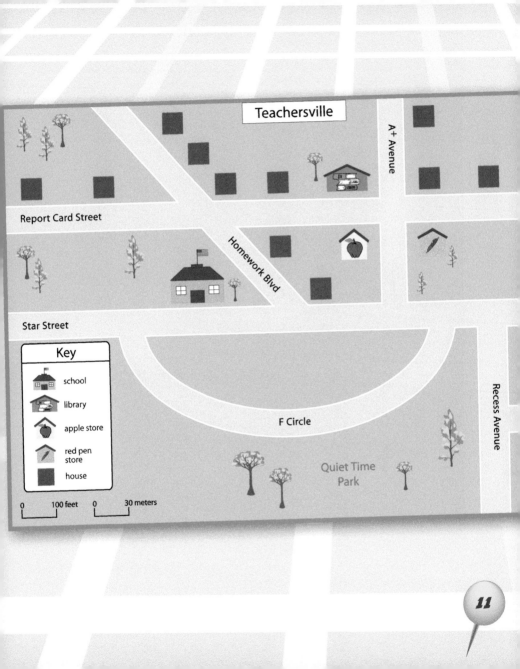

Road maps use black dots

to stand for cities.

Colored lines are roads.

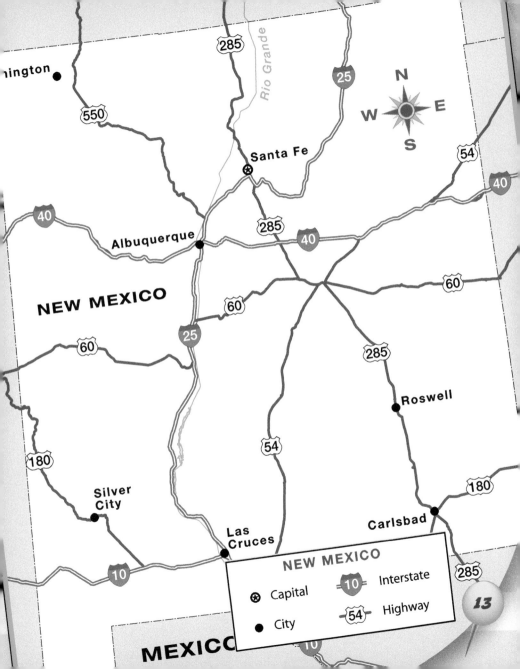

Maps of buildings
use shape symbols too.
Symbols show where
to find stairs or exits.

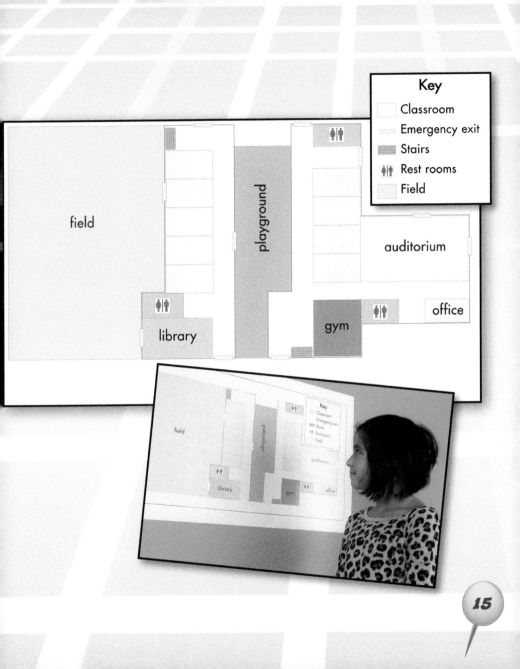

Key

Classroom
Emergency exit
Stairs
Rest rooms
Field

field

playground

auditorium

office

library

gym

Picture Symbols

Some maps use symbols
that look like
the things they stand for.
A sun stands for a sunny day
on a weather map.

National Forecast

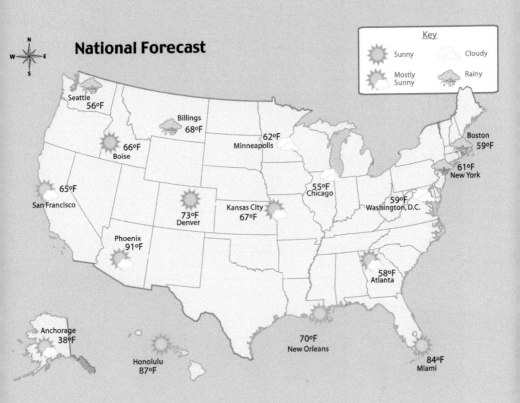

Key

Sunny   Cloudy

Mostly Sunny   Rainy

Seattle 56°F

Billings 68°F

62°F Minneapolis

Boston 59°F

66°F Boise

61°F New York

65°F San Francisco

55°F Chicago

59°F Washington, D.C.

73°F Denver

Kansas City 67°F

Phoenix 91°F

58°F Atlanta

Anchorage 38°F

Honolulu 87°F

70°F New Orleans

84°F Miami

Some maps even use

pictures as symbols.

A picture of a bear

on a zoo map

shows where the bears live.

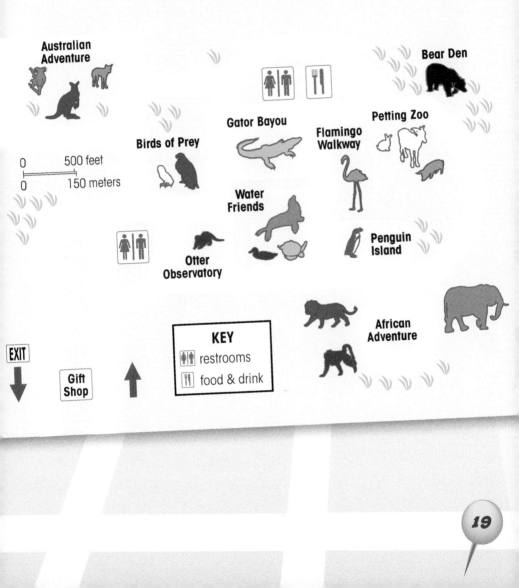

Australian Adventure

Bear Den

Gator Bayou

Petting Zoo

Birds of Prey

Flamingo Walkway

0   500 feet

0   150 meters

Water Friends

Otter Observatory

Penguin Island

African Adventure

EXIT

Gift Shop

KEY
restrooms
food & drink

19

Color Symbols

Colors can be symbols too.

Red can stand for hot weather.

Symbols really are a colorful,

helpful map tool.

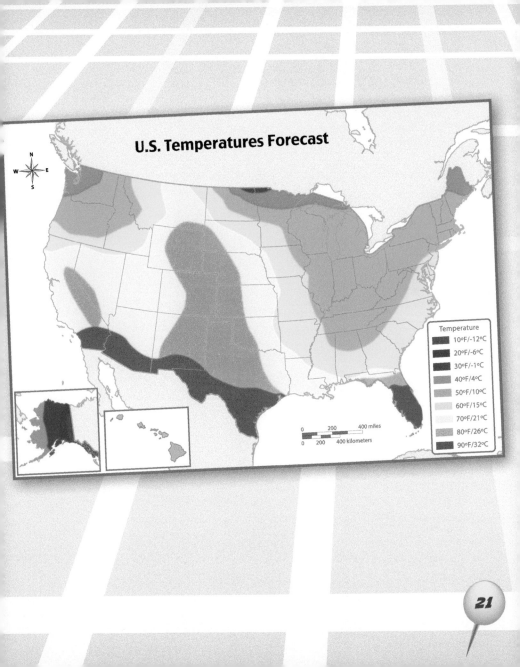

U.S. Temperatures Forecast

Temperature
10°F/-12°C
20°F/-6°C
30°F/-1°C
40°F/4°C
50°F/10°C
60°F/15°C
70°F/21°C
80°F/26°C
90°F/32°C

0   200   400 miles
0   200   400 kilometers

Glossary

chart—something that shows information in the form of a picture or graph

key—a list or chart that explains symbols on a map or graph

legend—a chart that explains symbols on a map; legend is another name for a map key

symbol—an object that stands for something else

weather—the condition outdoors at a certain time and place; weather changes with each season

Read More

Besel, Jennifer M. *Types of Maps*. Maps. North Mankato, Minn.: Capstone Press, 2014.

Greve, Meg. *Keys and Symbols on Maps*. Little World Geography. Vero Beach, Fla.: Rourke Pub., 2010.

Spilsbury, Louise. *Mapping*. Investigate. Chicago: Heinemann Library, 2010.

Internet Sites

FactHound offers a safe, fun way to find Internet sites related to this book. All of the sites on FactHound have been researched by our staff.

Here's all you do:

Visit *www.facthound.com*

Type in this code: 9781476530826

Critical Thinking Using the Common Core

1. Describe the steps to use a key to find a location on a map. (Key Ideas and Details)

2. Look at the maps on pages 13 and 19. What are some of the major differences and similarities between maps that use shape symbols and maps that use picture symbols? (Craft and Structure)

3. Look at the maps on pages 17 and 21. Both maps show information related to weather. Describe the differences between these maps. When would each of these maps be most useful? (Integration of Knowledge and Ideas)

Index

Word Count: 173
Grade: 1
Early-Intervention Level: 16